Feeding Minds
and
Touching Hearts

Spiritual Development in the
Primary School Project Report

The National Society's RE Centre
1996 – 1999

Project Directors
Alan Brown and Alison Seaman

A National Society Research Project based at the National Society's
RE Centre funded by All Saints Educational Trust.

Project reference number 208

The National Society
*Leading Education
with a Christian Purpose*
Church House Publishing

National Society/Church House Publishing
Church House
Great Smith Street
London SW1P 3NZ

ISBN 0 7151 4940 7

Published 2001 by National Society Enterprises Ltd

Copyright © The National Society (Church of England) for Promoting Religious Education 2001

Tel: 020 7898 1557
Fax: 020 7898 1449
Email: copyright@c-of-e.org.uk

Cover design by Julian Smith
Printed in England by Halstan & Co. Ltd, Amersham, Bucks

Contents

Acknowledgements

This National Society Research Project, based at the National Society's RE Centre, was funded by All Saints Educational Trust. The Project Directors are grateful to the Trust for their generous support. They are also indebted to the project's steering group and to teachers from the following schools who gave their time, creativity and commitment to the project.

Brant Broughton C of E/Methodist Primary School, Lincolnshire
Belmont Junior School, Durham
Compton C of E Primary School, Winchester
Dr Bell's and St Matthias College C of E Junior School, Bristol
Durdans Park Primary School, Southall, London
Esh C of E Primary School, Durham
Herne Junior School, Herne, Kent
Holy Trinity C of E Primary School, Yeovil, Somerset
Long Bennington C of E Primary School, Newark
Medstead C of E Primary School, Alton, Hampshire
Mundella County Primary School, Folkstone, Kent
Oaklands Primary School, Hanwell, London
Oak Trees County Primary School, Maidstone, Kent
Oliver Tomkins C of E Infant School, Swindon
Oliver Tomkins C of E Junior School, Swindon
Our Lady of the Visitation RC Primary School, Greenford, London
Potterhanworth C of E Primary School, Lincoln
St Bartholomew's Primary School, Coventry
St Gabriel's C of E Primary School, Pimlico, London
St James C of E (Voluntary Controlled) Primary School, Crigglestone, Wakefield
St John's C of E Middle School, Stanmore, Middlesex
St Mary's C of E Junior School, Basingstoke, Hampshire
St Paul's C of E Primary School, Leamington Spa, Warwickshire
St Paul's C of E Primary School, Whitechapel, London
St Paul's C of E Primary School, Newcastle upon Tyne
South Parade Infant School, Ossett, Wakefield
William Stukeley C of E Primary School, Holbeach, Lincolnshire

Freelance education consultant: Geoff Taggart

Project steering group: Lynne Broadbent, Mike Brownbill, Geoff Edwards, Robin Protheroe, Lilian Weatherley.

Preface

Feeding minds and touching hearts

A colleague was discussing his work, as a teacher, with the late Cardinal Basil Hume. 'What *is* education all about?' he asked of his wise mentor. After a brief pause came the thoughtful response, 'Feeding minds and touching hearts'. This powerful insight into the need for balance between head and heart in the education process encapsulated for us, as Project Directors, the work of the Spiritual Development Project and hence our decision to use these words as the title for the project report.

Alan Brown and Alison Seaman, Project Directors

Artwork by pupils of Herne Junior School, Kent. Pupils took part in a project designed to inspire a spiritual response. Art was used as the outward expression of internal feelings and/or experiences.

On   the   rough Seashore.
The   Sea   is   a   biting cat.
growling   at   the   Moon.

Ricky

Poem written as a response to a piece of music.

Picture drawn to the music of 'The Snowman'.

Introduction

Starting points

Compiling this report has been an opportunity to think back to the events that led to the establishment of the Spiritual Development Project. Inspiration came from a surprising number and range of different sources. We were given, for example, a quotation from Pearson's book, *Awakening the Heroes Within* (Harper, 1991). It read 'we are in sacred space all the time' and this captured our imagination when we considered the place of the spiritual in education. It seemed to us that in schools where the spiritual dimension was acknowledged and carefully nurtured, both pupil and teacher, independently and together, were given the opportunity to discover the power of the sacred – in time, in place and in people. It was as though sacred space had been created; there was opportunity for all in the school to rise above the ordinary and the everyday, to foster the development of the human spirit and to delight in the creativity offered by each learning experience.

But how can this process be described? It can be expressed using explicitly religious language, but for many teachers this is unsatisfactory and they want to find expression in purely secular terms. It is difficult to find words to articulate adequately what is happening. We were keen to find out more about how some schools seem to awaken spiritual awareness successfully. Is it something that 'just happens'? Can it be created given an appropriate toolkit? Is it easier to find in schools with a religious foundation?

Our use of the term 'sacred' immediately raises significant issues about terminology. The words 'sacred' and 'secular' both carry a baggage with them that has strong religious or non-religious overtones, making teachers anxious about using either term. Is there a need for a neutral language that can sit easily between the secular and sacred language found in everyday speech?

The Spiritual Development Project began by collecting together a group of teachers working in very different contexts and with very different teaching experiences. Over three years we explored together the spiritual dimension with all the joys and challenges that this inevitably brings. This report tries to record the processes and outcomes of our shared experiences and offers support materials to guide others who wish, themselves, to set out on this journey of exploration. You could begin by asking yourself, 'Are we in sacred space all the time...?'

My wonders ! ...

I wonder about every thing and how it was made

_e.g._

what are trees made out of
Seeds
what are seeds made Out of
and So on.

how did the first person
adam and eve get on
earth ?

A.D.Joynson

Poem written as a response to a piece of music.

Spiritual development in the primary school

Background

The word 'spiritual' has appeared in various Education Acts over the last 50 years since the Education Act 1944. This elusive word lay dormant and conveniently undefined until the Schools Inspection Act of 1992 created a situation in which the spiritual development of pupils would need to be inspected.

There is nothing quite like inspection to sharpen the minds and open the hearts of teachers (and indeed the inspectors themselves) to what 'spiritual' might mean. Early guidance from OFSTED, the Government's inspection agency, appeared to imply that the spiritual development of pupils could be measured in less than one week, i.e. during the length of the inspection. While teachers may well have prayed for a good inspection report, it was always unlikely that inspectors would be able to measure the spiritual development of pupils even if they were sure what 'spiritual development' meant and how it might be inspected.

The current guidance from OFSTED on inspecting spiritual development continues to be both obscure and obtuse. There is little clarity over what is meant by 'spiritual'. The inspection regime has suffered from a political decision in the 1940s to substitute the word 'religion' with the word 'spiritual' in the Education Act of 1944. Some OFSTED inspectors were and continue to be, apparently, very clear about what is meant by 'spiritual' but teachers and academics have been less easy to persuade of such clarity. Inspection of spiritual development in the early and mid-1990s became a charade when inspectors, quite correctly, inspected 'spiritual development' according to set criteria, but the criteria meant little and were not easily understood. This lack of clarity may be one reason why spiritual development continues to be taught less successfully than social or moral development and is commented on as such in the Chief Inspector's report for 1999.

The OFSTED model of inspection suggests that one can inspect spiritual development by fitting it into a definitive framework. In contrast to this, the wisdom of ages, from the world over, resists any clear and closed definition of the spiritual. Spirituality has always been glimpsed in the dreams and visions of saints, mystics and imaginative individuals, by people of faith, people of no faith, and from all cultures. The world's greatest mystics have recognized the limitations of language and have been confined within their social and cultural context and conventions.

> There was an overall feeling that we could appreciate the need to develop, or certainly nurture children's spirituality but there were doubts about what it actually was and how, therefore, it could be recognized within a school context. One teacher reflected that she was wary at first and thought it might be yet another thing to take on board. In fact it has been a development of things we already do.

OLIVER TOMKINS
INFANTS SCHOOL

It was with these thoughts in mind that the National Society, in 1996, invited the All Saints Educational Trust to share in an initiative that would support teachers and provide advice to those struggling with what was meant by 'spiritual development'. The aim was to encourage and enable schools to develop their understanding of what was meant by spiritual development and apply that understanding to pupils at Key Stages 1 and 2. Teachers and schools would have the opportunity to work together to create a broad framework within which a response to the 'spiritual development' inspection criteria could find proper expression. If such a framework could be created and rooted firmly in the school and in classroom practice, teachers would, it was intended, feel more confident and more able to support and guide pupils in the development of spiritual awareness.

The aims of the project

1. To provide schools with appropriate support materials for an exploration of spiritual development across the whole curriculum.

2. To provide schools with appropriate support materials for an exploration of the contribution made by the daily act of collective worship to spiritual development.

3. To create and publish appropriate resource materials for teachers and pupils in primary schools in the area of spiritual development.

Methodology

A range of different types of primary schools was identified with help from LEA and diocesan education advisers. The schools were in a variety of settings – urban, sub-urban and rural – and were in different areas of England (see page iv). Originally,

27 schools were contacted and visited by the Project Directors, and then took part in initial pilot studies. (A small number of these were unable to maintain their involvement in the project beyond the pilot stage because of staffing changes or the pressures of school inspection.) Each school then nominated a member of staff to focus on the project's activities and to coordinate work carried out in their school.

Over the three years of the project, activities included:

1. Working with teachers to develop an understanding of spiritual development within education.

2. Enabling teachers to apply their understanding of spiritual development to the requirements of the national curriculum, religious education and collective worship.

3. Preparing support materials for in-service training.

Specific schools would concentrate on particular areas of the curriculum in order to match teacher expertise and experience. The whole project would ensure comprehensive coverage of the national curriculum and religious education.

The process

The process of the project enabled and encouraged schools to develop their own awareness of what was meant by spiritual development. Each school was encouraged to explore the spiritual dimension in the way the staff felt was most appropriate and in line with their school development plan. The schools could also approach spiritual development in ways appropriate to their environment and school population. In practice, this meant that the headteacher, or another nominated member of staff, would take responsibility for joining the project, coordinate work carried out in their school and attend an annual conference organized by the Project Directors. The conferences played a significant part in supporting members of the project in their work and in helping to develop a deeper understanding of the spiritual dimension in education. The project was, however, essentially a practical

The Spiritual Development Project has helped us to focus on what *is* spiritual development and to look at ways of allowing it to happen within the school day. It has helped us to listen to the children's responses with acceptance rather than trying to give them the answer.

OLIVER TOMKINS
INFANTS SCHOOL

piece of work. There was, of course, a theoretical foundation underpinning the developments in each school, but, the emphasis of the project was always focused on what was, is, could, or should be put into effect in a primary school.

The project was launched and visits were made to all the schools. Staff in a small number of schools were diffident or anxious. Some members of staff were unsure of what would be required of them and how they might be able to respond if asked to participate. The momentum grew, however, and schools began to think about ways in which they could explore spiritual development. The project representatives coordinated and monitored the activities carried out in their school and, at the project's annual conferences, opportunity was given to explore together and reflect upon the work that was being done.

Each school, not surprisingly, started to explore spiritual development in the area where it felt most confident or where it considered most work needed to be done. Some schools worked in the creative arts using dance, drama, music and puppetry; others mapped the curriculum to look for opportunities for spiritual development. Some created books of stories, poetry and artwork produced by the children; others used the opportunity to work with the governing body to explore what 'spiritual development' might be. Some used in-service days to accelerate thinking and took time to reconsider the management and organization of the school.

> We felt our starting point should be the curriculum. We drew up a curriculum map identifying opportunities for spiritual development. The important spin-off from this work was to make us more aware that a lot was already being done to promote the children's spiritual development. We became more aware of the potential of all the curriculum areas for spiritual development. Previously we had just focused our ideas on RE and Worship.

Esh C of E
PRIMARY
School

It is important to acknowledge that, while the teachers who attended the project conferences were interested in the area of spiritual development, their colleagues back at school did not always share their enthusiasm. These events, therefore, provided a forum for feedback and sharing ideas, and a chance to develop new ideas and thinking in the area of spiritual development. It was an opportunity to work with others who valued the place of the spiritual dimension in education. Wide-ranging views were exchanged, and there was by no means a consensus of opinion, but participants welcomed the opportunity to look, in depth, at the issues surrounding the debate about spiritual development. One significant thread that ran through the project looked at the secular and religious approaches to spiritual development in schools. The first conference, for example, explored various aspects of what could be meant by 'spiritual'. Attention was drawn to the fact that in our discussions there had been little mention of 'God'.

With that in mind the second conference began with a reflection on religious and secular interpretations of spiritual development. The issue, oversimplified here, was that whilst one can talk about music, natural beauty, technological skills and creating a spiritual atmosphere, and about children's spirituality, where does God fit into the discussion? Can one engage with the spiritual without engaging with God? Is the emphasis on spirituality simply a convenience to ensure that mention of God and belief in God can be set aside? It was, in effect, a reflection on the question of whether one can have a spiritual experience that is distinct from an aesthetic experience. Some tensions emerged around the different approaches to God and the way in which spiritual development was, or was not, related to religious development and understanding. Some of these tensions were then creatively explored by John Hammond from St Martin's College, Lancaster, who led the third conference.

Some reflections on the process

The work of the Spiritual Development Project would, in conclusion, have a variety of consequences. One school changed its whole approach to spiritual development and the project took off like a flame in dry brushwood, affecting the ethos of the school and its whole approach to teaching. In another example, the project affected the headteacher and through her, and the way in which she organized and conducted worship, the whole school benefited, but in an indirect way.

Inevitably the project had greater influence and success in some schools than in others but, most significantly, there was a growth in confidence among teachers in tackling the area of spiritual development. Participating in the project gave them the opportunity to find expression for their ideas and ways of describing the spiritual dimension. The very obscurity of the term 'spiritual development' became a strength, producing a rich diversity of approaches, all of which tapped into the creative imagination of both teachers and pupils.

Over the course of the three years some views emerged about the challenges faced by schools in the area of spiritual development. These are outlined here.

1.   Working with the prevailing 'culture' in education

There is no denying that the education system in England has experienced considerable change in the last ten to fifteen years. New legislation with accompanying documentation arrived thick and fast on the desk of every teacher and headteacher. The regular round of inspections, together with the arrival of league tables, target setting and performance management has created an education system focused upon raising standards, value for money and the 'successful' or 'failing' school. Project members identified the ways in which the prevailing culture in education can militate against the spirit of the school:

- the pressure associated with school inspections;

- the speed and extent of changes in education, which can lead to heads and teachers feeling 'shell-shocked' and overloaded;

- the impact of curriculum changes and a greater emphasis on prescribed teaching methods, e.g. the literacy and numeracy strategies; working with an overloaded curriculum. A particular concern was the pressure on time for activities that encourage pupils to use their imagination and creativity, e.g. in the creative arts, PE and games.

2.   Please, no more 'add-ons'!

Project members were clear that spiritual development should underpin the whole curriculum, collective worship and the ethos of the school. Treating it as another 'add-on' to an already overloaded curriculum was unhelpful. Some schools, for example, had tried to add a space for notes on spiritual development to their planning documents. This, however, was found to be a rather contrived approach and could lead to tokenism. A shared understanding of spiritual development by all staff in the school and an awareness of the ways in which the spiritual dimension can be nurtured, ensured that the spiritual dimension underpinned all aspects of school life rather than just being an added extra.

3.   The spirit of the teacher

As with all diverse groups of people, the members of the Spiritual Development Project held differing views about the nature of the spiritual dimension. One of the uniting influences, which brought widespread agreement, was the importance of nurturing the spirit of the teacher.

Alongside this viewpoint, which places the person of the teacher as paramount, came the understanding that the nurture of the spirit of the teacher was as important as that of the child. Indeed, it was difficult to see how the latter could happen without the former. This, however, places considerable responsibility on the head and the governing body to ensure that teachers' needs are catered for when nurturing the spiritual dimension of a school.

Probably the greatest impact of the project for me was on a personal level. I think that the development of spirituality in a school can only happen if the staff feel comfortable about 'being spiritual'. Part of the headteacher's role is to help the staff towards that confidence. The project made me think about spirituality and the many ways it can be expressed and experienced. It reinforced for me the central importance of spirituality in developing the child as a whole person.

COMPTON C OF E
PRIMARY SCHOOL

4.   Not religious but spiritual . . .

It was recognized by many of the teachers in project schools that, although they would not describe themselves as 'religious', they would consider themselves to be 'spiritual'. The view is often expressed that while people wish to distance themselves from 'religion' they are at pains to stress their spirituality by speaking of a personal ethical stance, meditative path and so on.

It was also recognized that there were teachers who felt profoundly uncomfortable with any discussion of the spiritual, wishing to identify the spiritual dimension as a personal matter. It is important to emphasize here that any discussion of the spiritual explores areas of human experience that are personal, can be painful and often require a recognition of one's vulnerability as well as one's strengths. Those who lead training sessions about spiritual development should be prepared for a bumpy ride! Also it should be borne in mind that people vary in their ability to articulate their views and feelings about the spiritual dimension. This is the case with both adults and children and it is important to be alive to the many different ways in which people express their spirituality.

5. Developing a shared understanding of spiritual development

The debate about religious and secular interpretations of the spiritual was live throughout the project. It often became polarized. There were those who felt this issue could only be clarified by identifying a definition of spiritual development. Again there were many differing views on this from which the following guidance emerged:

- It is important for schools to come to a shared understanding of spiritual development in their community.

- Teachers and school governors need to develop a shared language to discuss and develop their ideas about the spiritual and to reach a common understanding of spiritual development.

- While some schools may wish to attempt to define spiritual development, project members felt that a range of descriptions was probably more helpful. These descriptions could form the basis of a school policy on spiritual development and might also make a significant contribution to formulating the school's mission statement.

We now want to work on a policy for spiritual development that involves all the staff. Our first step has been to collect together pieces of the children's work that we feel identify some aspect of spiritual development. This helps us to make it visible and to describe it rather than saying 'it's just there'.

POTTERHANWORTH
C OF E PRIMARY
SCHOOL

Reflections

Two members of the Spiritual Development Project's Steering Group give their reflections on the project.

Lynne Broadbent, Director, BFSS RE Centre, Brunel University

'What does the word "spiritual" mean to you?'

This was the challenge posed by the Steering Group for the first residential conference of the project. And it was indeed a real challenge! For those of us familiar with the *Discussion Papers on Spiritual and Moral Development* (OFSTED, 1994 and NCC, 1993) there was a strong temptation to resort to the anonymity of their descriptions and definitions. However, devoid of such crutches, members of the conference confronted the intensely personal, and sometimes moving, events and relationships that mark a human life.

A second session confirmed the need to address the question from a personal perspective when participants were asked to evaluate definitions of 'the spiritual' from faith and educational sources. Most agreed, with relief, that 'what the teacher is, is as important as what the teacher knows', and pondered over Ursula King's statement that the spiritual is 'a response to life; a struggle for life . . . in essence active and developmental, involving the whole person'. ('Recovering a lost dimension', *BJRE*, 1985.)

Pressure from teachers on the project persuaded a member of the Steering Group to present a perspective on the spiritual by reference to Scripture. This presentation, during the second residential conference, was a *tour de force*, exploring a universalist approach to biblical text, from Abraham, Ruth, Jonah and the Psalms to Jesus and St Paul, and including reference to Hindu and Sikh concepts. Some participants found meaning in the exploration, others strongly disputed this particular interpretation of Scripture.

There were opportunities to listen to children's voices, comments from classrooms where reception children had transformed the home corner into a 'special place' with rules for its use and where a whole school had explored the changing wonders of the natural world through music and image. And there was silence; opportunities to participate in brief periods of focused meditation, loosely based upon Christian meditative practice.

11

The interplay between personal experience, exploring the written word, sacred and secular, listening to voices of pupils and opportunities to participate in silence, discussion and dispute, both shaped the project and made it a valuable learning experience for teachers, pupils and members of the Steering Group alike. Many of us would wish to identify succinctly the contribution made by the curriculum areas and collective worship to pupils' spiritual development and to fix the 'formula' within a policy statement. However, if the spiritual is, as Ursula King suggests, 'dynamic, energising and transforming', then it is the process of active and ongoing exploration, modelled by the project itself, which may best serve each generation of teachers as they struggle to identify sound and educational provision for pupils' spiritual development.

Geoff Edwards, Adviser, London Diocesan Board for Schools

From the very beginning of the project, it was clear that schools, and what was happening in classrooms, were central to the project's thinking. They were also critical for the success of the project. The aims spoke of developing understanding and of supporting and enabling teachers.

One of the project's strengths was the variety of schools and contexts that were represented. This became apparent in the conferences that were held for the participating schools. For me, the conferences were important because I was able to hear teachers discuss their experiences of engaging with spiritual development across the curriculum. What was vital was that these experiences, and the work that developed from them, were grounded in day-to-day interactions in classrooms.

Alongside these practical approaches were more theoretical presentations and discussions. Frequently, these were thought-provoking and challenging. My personal challenge was to talk briefly about spiritual values in school management despite an initial cynicism that this was an area where there was little time for reflection and precious little 'awe and wonder'!

The shared experience from the project's schools showed that there is some outstanding developmental work being carried out across the country. This work is being shared further, as project schools network with each other and act as resources for teachers in their own areas.

The success of the project will be twofold: firstly, the collaboration of the project schools as they work together, and secondly, the dissemination stage when the ideas and advice emanating from the project are taken up in primary schools nationally. All the evidence so far suggests that primary schools want this support. The project report provides the groundwork and inspiration to enable schools to work through the same process and creatively explore this significant area of school life.

So what is spiritual development...?

Training activities for teachers, governors and parents

The following activities were piloted and developed during the Spiritual Development Project and are offered as a set of materials to support schools in developing a shared understanding of the spiritual dimension in education. While each activity will stand alone, activities one, two and three are best followed through in sequence and provide a foundation for a deeper exploration of spiritual development.

Activity one (page 15)

Begin by asking, 'If you could give your child one gift or quality when s/he leaves school, what would it be?' (see page 15). Ask participants to write down their gift, then on a flip chart collect together some examples from the group. The gifts usually include some of the following: a positive self-esteem, confidence, honesty, happiness, respect for others. Discuss together where the development of such gifts can take place in school life.

Activity two (page 16)

There has been very little guidance offered from government bodies to help schools explore the spiritual dimension in education. Work through some or all of the areas identified in *Spiritual and Moral Development – A Discussion Paper*, NCC (now QCA), 1993 (see page 16). This activity stimulates discussion about religious and secular interpretations of spiritual development.

Activity three (page 17)

Use the grid of quotations about spiritual development (see page 17). You could substitute examples of your own. Ask participants to identify those descriptions or statements with which they either agree or disagree. This is usually best done in twos or threes, depending on the size of the group. Ask groups to feedback. This is a significant stage of the process because a shared understanding of spiritual development can begin to emerge from the group at this stage.

Activity four (pages 18, 19, 20, 21)

During one of the project conferences, we looked at different aspects of school life to try to identify significant areas that can contribute to pupils' spiritual development. These comments and ideas were then collected together and grouped into four areas under the general heading of 'Teachers Talking about Spiritual Development . . .' (see pages 18–21). Use them to help identify opportunities for spiritual development in your school.

Our experience when piloting these materials has been that teachers find it helpful to identify areas of their own work where they are already providing opportunities for spiritual development. The strength of listening to the voices of other teachers is in helping to build confidence in working with the spiritual dimension and to take away something of the 'mystique' associated with spiritual development.

If you could give

your child one gift

or quality when s/he

leaves school

what

would it be?

_____

From Burns, S and Lamont, G (1995)

Aspects of spiritual development

Beliefs

A sense of awe, wonder and mystery

Experiencing feelings of transcendence

Search for meaning and purpose

Self-knowledge

Relationships

Creativity

Feelings and emotions

From *Spiritual and Moral Development – A Discussion Paper*,
NCC (now QCA), 1993.

Spiritual development

Curriculum is one half of the education process, the other half is the people concerned in that process. To reduce the educational discussion to 'curriculum' is not only to strain the language. It means that certain aspects of education are missing.	What is spiritual takes on a quality of something ultimately impenetrable, of what must forever remain a mystery, although it can be explored.	An educator's role is to educate. Spiritual development is to do with the priest.
We are in sacred space all the time.	Spiritual development relates to that aspect of inner life through which pupils acquire insights into their personal existence, which are of enduring worth.	All curriculum areas have a positive contribution to make to the school's provision of opportunities for spiritual development.
What the teacher is, is as important as what the teacher knows . . .	'Spiritual' is not synonymous with 'religious'.	It is not the role of the school to inculcate spiritual values in a secular society.

Teachers talking about spiritual development . . .

Some implications for schools

- Children need time for reflection – to be fascinated by the simple discoveries they make.

- It is important to value children's observations of their world – including responses to the ordinary and the everyday.

- We should not shy away from asking or exploring 'unanswerable' questions.

- It is important to help children develop appropriate skills and attitudes, e.g. reflection, stillness, observation, learning to value and respect the experience of others.

- Staff are significant role models; their attitudes and awareness will filter through to the children.

- Although spiritual development can come from spontaneous situations, schools should have basic structures and resources in place to promote it.

Teachers talking about spiritual development . . .

Management and leadership issues

The importance of the following was identified:

- A shared vision for the school and shared values.

- Working together to achieve agreed goals.

- Establishing a community where all are valued and where there is a strong commitment to build sound relationships between staff, between pupils, and between staff and pupils.

- Consistency of approach, e.g. in behaviour policy, in the way staff respond to children.

- To have a shared understanding of spiritual development leading to a clear policy that is 'owned' by all: children, staff, governors, parents.

- Planning to allow opportunities for spontaneity.

Teachers talking about spiritual development . . .

Classroom strategies

- Provide opportunities for active learning.

- Circle time can be a useful forum for the expression of personal feelings.

- Class worship can build a sense of belonging.

- Time should be found for confidential support and opportunities for children to communicate with the teacher. Have a 'worry box' or post box, for messages during busy times.

- Celebrate children's work and ideas using interesting and/or interactive displays. Try to draw attention to detail.

- Group children to cultivate sound relationships.

- Build into the timetable opportunity for reflection and stillness. Use a candle or other object to signal quiet times.

- Provide opportunities for children to share their experiences. Be prepared for these not always to be pleasant ones. Difficult times and crises can make a significant contribution to spiritual development.

Teachers talking about spiritual development . . .

Teaching styles

- Build good relationships with pupils, e.g. through openness, a sense of humour, a willingness to listen, being consistent, developing trust.

- Value each individual.

- Have a wide range of teaching strategies at your fingertips; what works for one does not necessarily work for another.

- Use open questions.

- Encourage children to be independent.

- Be prepared to be childlike to experience the joys and thrills felt by the children.

- Bring enriching experiences into the day-to-day curriculum.

- Use role-play to encourage the children to 'stand in someone else's shoes'.

- Remember that teachers also need to be seen to be learners.

Bibliography

Best, R (ed.), *Education, Spirituality and the Whole Child*, Cassell, 1996.

Brown, A and Furlong, J, *Spiritual Development in Schools*, The National Society, 1996.

Burns, S and Lamont, G, *Values and Visions*, Hodder and Stoughton, 1995.

Catholic Education Service, *Spiritual and Moral Development Across the Whole Curriculum*, CES, 1995.

Hay, D and Nye R, *The Spirit of the Child*, Fount, 1998.

Kent County Council, *Shaping the Spiritual – Promoting the Spiritual Development of Young People in Schools*, Kent County Council, 1999.

King, Ursula, 'Recovering a lost dimension', *British Journal of Religious Education*, Vol. 7, No. 3, 1985.

Lewisham Education Service, *SMSC – Providing for Spiritual, Moral, Social and Cultural Development of Pupils*, Lewisham Education Service, 1999.

Mackley, J, *Looking Inwards, Looking Outwards*, Christian Education Movement, 1997.

NCC, *Spiritual and Moral Development – A Discussion Paper*, NCC, 1993.

OFSTED, *Spiritual, Moral, Social and Cultural Development*. An OFSTED Discussion Paper, HMSO, 1994.

OFSTED, The Annual Report of Her Majesty's Inspector of Schools, HMSO, 2000.

Pearson, C, *Awakening the Heroes Within*, Harper, 1991.

Priestley, J, 'Towards finding the hidden curriculum: a consideration of the spiritual dimension of experience in curriculum planning', *British Journal of Religious Education*, Vol. 7, No. 3, 1985.

SCAA, *Education for Adult Life; the spiritual and moral development of young people*, SCAA, 1996.

Smith, D, *Making Sense of Spiritual Development*, The Stapleford Centre, 1999.

Stone, M , *Don't Just Do Something, Sit There*, RMEP, 1995.

Webster, D, 'A spiritual dimension for education', in Francis and Thatcher (eds) *Christian Perspectives for Education*, Gracewing, 1995.

Underwater Miracles

I think that sea life, under the summer waters, is a summer miracle, with the sea changing colour all the time. The dolphins splashing, the sun shining on their smooth bodies. The gentle waves lapping up on to the beach, and the tropical fish swimming silently. I think that this is one of gods best miracle as it is mysterious and exciting.

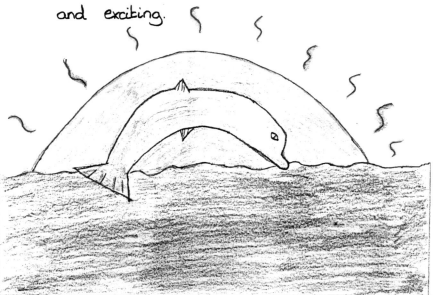

By Abigail Williams

Poem written as a response to a spiritual development project using music.

Picture response to an assembly on 'Earth, Sea and Sky'.